THE
BARBECUE
AND GRILL
BOOK

THE
BARBECUE
AND GRILL
BOOK

SIZZLING IDEAS FOR
DELICIOUS OUTDOOR EATING

Consultant Editor: Christine France

HERMES
HOUSE

This edition produced in 2001 by Hermes House

©Anness Publishing Ltd 2001

Hermes House is an imprint of Anness Publishing Limited
Hermes House, 88–89 Blackfriars Road, London SE1 8HA

A CIP catalogue record for this book is available from the British Library

Publisher: Joanna Lorenz
Project Editor: Linda Doeser
Copy Editor: Beverley Jollands
Designers: Nigel Partridge, Siân Keogh
Illustrations: Madeleine David and Lucinda Ganderton
Front cover: Lisa Tai, Designer; Thomas Odulate, Photographer;
Helen Trent, Stylist; Lucy McKelvie, Home Economist
Photographers: Karl Adamson, William Adams-Lingwood, Edward Allwright, Steve
Baxter, James Duncan, John Freeman, Michelle Garrett, Amanda Heywood, Don Last,
Michael Michaels, Patrick McLeavey, Debbie Patterson and Juliet Piddington
Recipes: Carla Capalbo, Jacqueline Clark, Carole Clements, Roz Denny, Nicola Diggins,
Tessa Evelegh, Joanna Farrow, Christine France, Silvana Franco, Soheila Kimberley, Ruby
Le Bois, Sue Maggs, Katherine Richmond, Steven Wheeler
and Elizabeth Wolf-Cohen

Previously published as part of a larger compendium, *The Ultimate Barbecue Cookbook*

Printed and bound in Hong Kong/China

1 3 5 7 9 10 8 6 4 2

NOTES
For all recipes, quantities are given in both metric and imperial measures, and, where
appropriate, measures are also given in standard cups and spoons. Follow one set, but not
a mixture, because they are not interchangeable.
Standard spoon and cup measurements are level.
1 tsp = 5ml, 1 tbsp = 15ml; 1 cup = 250ml/8fl oz
Australian standard tablespoons are 20 ml. Australian readers should use 3 tsp in place of
1 tbsp for measuring small quantities of gelatine, cornflour, salt, etc.
Medium eggs should be used unless otherwise specified.

CONTENTS

o o o

INTRODUCTION

...

Cooking outdoors is one of the great pleasures of the summer. The delicious smell of char-grilling food is almost irresistible, stimulates the appetite and – even better – tempts everyone to help with the cooking.

The recipes in this book are divided into six chapters with something for all tastes, each course and every occasion. Five-spice Rib-stickers, Shish Kebab, Spiced Beef Satay and Blackened Cajun Chicken and Corn feature among the all-time favourites, and there are many innovative and unusual barbecue treats. These include Lamb Burgers with Redcurrant Chutney, Grilled Sea Bass with Citrus Fruit and Barbecued Goat's Cheese Pizza. Plenty of vegetarian dishes are included and barbecued desserts will be a delicious new taste experience for those who have never thought of char-grilling fruit.

The introductory section of the book is packed with helpful information to make cooking on a barbecue as trouble-free, safe and relaxed as possible. It includes advice on the various types of barbecue, kinds of charcoal and other fuels, safety tips, cooking times and marinating.

Whether you are planning a family picnic with a disposable barbecue or throwing a summer party with a sophisticated gas grill, you will find that cooking this way makes food taste better, while also being fun and easy to prepare.

CHOOSING A BARBECUE

There is a huge choice of ready-made barbecues on the market, and it's important to choose one that suits your needs. First decide how many people you want to cook for and where you are likely to use the barbecue. For instance, do you usually have barbecues just for the family, or are you likely to have barbecue parties for lots of friends? Once you've decided on your basic requirements, you will be able to choose between the different types more easily.

Hibachi Barbecues

These small cast-iron barbecues originated in Japan – the word *hibachi* translates literally as 'firebox'. They are inexpensive, easy to use and easily transportable. Lightweight versions are now made in steel or aluminium.

ABOVE: *Hibachi barbecue*

Disposable Barbecues

These will last for about an hour and are a convenient idea for picnic-style barbecues or for cooking just a few small pieces of food.

Portable Barbecues

These are usually quite light and fold away to fit into a car boot so you can take them on picnics. Some are even small enough to fit into a rucksack.

Brazier Barbecues

These open barbecues are suitable for use on a patio or in the garden. Most have legs or wheels and it's a good idea to check that the height suits you. The grill area of a brazier barbecue varies in size and the barbecue may be round or rectangular. It's useful to choose one that has a shelf attached to the side. Other extras may include an electric, battery-powered or clockwork spit: choose one on which you can adjust the height of the spit. Many brazier barbecues have a hood, which is useful as a windbreak and gives a place to mount the spit.

LEFT: *Brazier barbecue*
BELOW: *Disposable barbecue*
RIGHT: *Portable barbecue*

ABOVE: Gas barbecue

Kettle-grill Barbecues

These have a large, hinged lid which can be used as a windbreak; when closed, the lid allows you to use the barbecue rather like an oven. Even large joints of meat or whole turkeys cook successfully, as the heat reflected within the dome helps to brown the meat evenly. The heat is easily controlled by the use of efficient air vents. This type of barbecue can also be used for home-smoking foods.

Gas Barbecues

The main advantage of these is their convenience – the heat is instant and easily controllable. The disadvantage is that they tend to be quite expensive.

Permanent Barbecues

These are a good idea if you often have barbecues at home. They can be built simply and cheaply. Choose a sheltered site that is a little way from the house, but with easy access to the kitchen. Permanent barbecues can be built with ordinary house bricks, but it's best to line the inside with firebricks, which will withstand the heat better. Use a metal shelf for the fuel and a grid at whatever height you choose. Packs are available containing all you need to build a barbecue.

Improvised Barbecues

Barbecue cooking adds to the fun of eating outdoors on picnics and camping trips but transporting the barbecue for the rest of the day can make the idea more of a chore than a treat. Basic barbecues can be built at almost no cost and can be dismantled after use as quickly as they were put together. A pile of stones topped with chicken wire and fuelled with driftwood or kindling makes a very efficient barbecue. Or take a large biscuit tin with you and punch a few holes in it; fill it with charcoal and place a grid on top. With just a little planning, you can turn your trip into a truly memorable event.

ABOVE: Improvised barbecue

ABOVE: Permanent barbecue

TYPES OF FUEL

. . .

If you have a gas or electric barbecue, you will not need to buy extra fuel, but other barbecues require either charcoal or wood. Choose good-quality fuel from sustainable sources, and always store it in a dry place.

Lumpwood Charcoal
Lumpwood charcoal is usually made from softwood, and comes in lumps of varying size. It is easier to ignite than briquettes, but tends to burn up faster.

Charcoal Briquettes
Briquettes are a cost-effective choice of fuel as they burn for a long time with the minimum of smell and smoke. They can take a long time to ignite, however.

ABOVE: Charcoal briquettes

Self-igniting Charcoal
This is simply lumpwood charcoal or briquettes, treated with a flammable substance that catches light very easily. It's important to wait until the ignition agent has burnt off before cooking food, or the smell may taint the food.

Coconut-shell Charcoal
This makes a good fuel for small barbecues. It's best used on a fire grate with small holes, as the small pieces tend to fall through the gaps.

Wood
Hardwoods such as oak and olive are best for barbecues, as they burn slowly with a pleasant aroma. Softwoods tend to burn too fast and give off sparks and smoke, making them unsuitable for most barbecues. Wood fires need constant attention to achieve an even, steady heat.

BELOW: Lumpwood

CONTROLLING THE HEAT
There are three basic ways to control the heat of the barbecue during cooking.

1 Adjust the height of the grill rack. Raise it for slow cooking, or use the bottom level for searing foods. For a medium heat, the rack should be about 10cm/4in from the fire.

2 Push the burning coals apart for a lower heat; pile them closer together to increase the heat of the fire.

3 Most barbecues have air vents to allow air into the fire. Open them to make the fire hotter, or close them to lower the temperature.

Woodchips and Herbs
These are designed to be added to the fire to impart a pleasant aroma to the food. They can be soaked to make them last longer. Scatter woodchips and herbs straight on to the coals during cooking, or place them on a metal tray under the grill rack. Packs of hickory or oak chips are easily available, or you can simply scatter twigs of juniper, rosemary, thyme, sage or fennel over the fire.

BELOW: Coconut shell

LIGHTING THE FIRE
Follow these basic instructions for lighting the fire unless you are using self-igniting charcoal, in which case you should follow the manu-facturer's instructions.

1 Spread a layer of foil over the base of the barbecue, to reflect the heat and make cleaning easier.

2 Spread a layer of wood, charcoal or briquettes on the fire grate about 5cm/2in deep. Pile the fuel in a small pyramid in the centre.

3 Push one or two firelighters into the pyramid or pour over about 45ml/3 tbsp liquid firelighter and leave for 1 minute. Light with a long match or taper and leave to burn for 15 minutes. Spread the coals evenly and leave for 30–45 minutes, until they are covered with a film of grey ash, before cooking.

SAFETY TIPS

. . .

Barbecuing is a perfectly safe method of cooking if it's done sensibly – use these simple guidelines as a basic checklist to safeguard against accidents. If you have never organized a barbecue before, keep your first few attempts as simple as possible, with just one or two types of food. When you have mastered the technique of cooking on a barbecue you can start to become more ambitious. Soon you will progress from burgers for two to meals for large parties of family and friends.

☆ Make sure the barbecue is sited on a firm surface and is stable and level before lighting the fire. Once the barbecue is lit, do not move it.

☆ Keep the barbecue sheltered from the wind, and keep it well away from trees and shrubs.

☆ Always follow the manufacturer's instructions for your barbecue, as there are some barbecues that can use only one type of fuel.

☆ Don't try to hasten the fire – some fuels may take quite a time to build up heat. Never pour flammable liquid on to the barbecue.

☆ Keep children and pets away from the fire and make sure the cooking is always supervised by adults.

☆ Keep perishable foods cold until you're ready to cook – especially in hot weather. If you take them outdoors, place them in a cool bag until needed.

☆ Make sure meats such as burgers, sausages and poultry are thoroughly cooked – there should be no trace of pink in the juices. Pierce a thick part of flesh as a test: the juices should run clear.

RIGHT: Poultry can be pre-cooked in the oven or microwave, before being finished off on the barbecue.

ABOVE: Light the fire with a long match or taper, and leave it to burn for about 15 minutes.

☆ Wash your hands after handling raw meat and before touching other foods. Don't use the same utensils for raw ingredients and cooked food.

☆ You may prefer to pre-cook poultry in the microwave or oven and then transfer it to the barbecue to finish off cooking and to attain the flavour of barbecued food. Don't allow meat to cool down before transferring it to the barbecue; poultry should never be reheated once it has cooled.

☆ In case the fire should get out of control, have a bucket of sand and a water spray on hand to douse the flames.

☆ Keep a first-aid kit handy. If someone burns themselves, hold the burn under cold running water.

☆ Trim excess fat from meat and don't use too much oil in marinades. Fat can cause dangerous flare-ups if too much is allowed to drip on to the fuel.

☆ Use long-handled barbecue tools, such as forks, tongs and brushes, for turning and basting food; keep some oven gloves to hand, preferably the extra-long type, to protect your hands.

☆ Always keep the raw foods to be cooked away from foods that are ready to eat, to prevent cross-contamination.

BASIC TIMING GUIDE

. . .

It is almost impossible to give precise timing guides for barbecue cooking as there are so many factors to consider. The heat will depend on the type and size of barbecue, the type of fuel used, the height of the grill above the fire and, of course, the weather. Cooking times will also be affected by the thickness and type of food, the quality of the meat, and whereabouts on the grill it is placed.

Bearing this in mind, the chart below provides only a rough guide to timing. Food should aways be tested to make sure it is thoroughly cooked. The times given here are total cooking time, allowing for the food to be turned. Most foods need turning only once but smaller items, such as kebabs and sausages, need to be turned more frequently to ensure even cooking. Foods wrapped in foil cook more slowly and will need longer on the barbecue.

Type of Food	Weight/ Thickness	Heat	Total Cooking Time
Beef			
steaks	2.5cm/1in	hot	rare: 5 minutes
			medium: 8 minutes
			well done: 12 minutes
burgers	2cm/¾ in	hot	6–8 minutes
kebabs	2.5cm/1in	hot	5–8 minutes
joints	1.5kg/3½ lb	spit	2–3 hours
Lamb			
leg steaks	2cm/¾ in	medium	10–15 minutes
chops	2.5cm/1in	medium	10–15 minutes
kebabs	2.5cm/1in	medium	6–15 minutes
butterfly leg	7.5cm/3in	low	rare: 40–45 minutes
			well done: 1 hour
rolled shoulder	1.5kg/3½ lb	spit	1¼–1½ hours
Pork			
chops	2.5cm/1in	medium	15–18 minutes
kebabs	2.5cm/1in	medium	12–15 minutes
spare ribs		medium	30–40 minutes
sausages	thick	medium	8–10 minutes
joints	1.5kg/3½ lb	spit	2–3 hours

Type of Food	Weight/ Thickness	Heat	Total Cooking Time
Chicken			
whole	1.5kg/3½ lb	spit	1–1¼ hours
quarters		medium	30–35 minutes
boneless breasts		medium	10–15 minutes
drumsticks		medium	25–30 minutes
kebabs		medium	6–10 minutes
poussin, whole	450g/1lb	spit	25–30 minutes
poussin, spatchcocked	450g/1lb	medium	25–30 minutes
Duckling			
whole	2.25kg/5lb	spit	1–1½ hours
half		medium	35–45 minutes
breasts, boneless		medium	15–20 minutes
Fish			
large, whole	2.25–4.5kg/ 5–10lb	low/ medium	allow 10 minutes per 2.5cm/1in thickness
small, whole	500–900g/ 1¼–2lb	hot/ medium	12–20 minutes
sardines		hot/ medium	4–6 minutes
steaks or fillets	2.5cm/1in	medium	6–10 minutes
kebabs	2.5cm/1in	medium	5–8 minutes
large prawns in shell		medium	6–8 minutes
large prawns, shelled		medium	4–6 minutes
scallops/mussels in shell		medium	until open
scallops/mussels, shelled, skewered		medium	5–8 minutes
half lobster		low/ medium	15–20 minutes

MARINATING

Marinades are used to add flavour and to moisten or tenderize foods, particularly meat. Marinades can be either savoury or sweet and are as varied as you want to make them: spicy, fruity, fragrant or exotic. Certain classic combinations always work well with certain foods. Usually, it is best to choose oily marinades for dry foods, such as lean meat or white fish, and wine- or vinegar-based marinades for rich foods with a higher fat content. Most marinades don't contain salt, which can draw out the juices from meat. It's better to add salt just before, or after, cooking.

1 Place the food for marinating in a wide, non-metallic dish or bowl, preferably a dish that is large enough to allow the food to lie in a single layer.

2 Mix together the ingredients for the marinade according to the recipe. The marinade can usually be prepared in advance and stored in a jar with a screw-top lid until needed.

3 Pour the marinade over the food and turn the food to coat it evenly.

4 Cover the dish or bowl with clear film and chill in the fridge for anything from 30 minutes up to several hours or overnight, depending on the recipe. Turn the food over occasionally and spoon the marinade over it to ensure it is well coated.

5 Remove the food with a slotted spoon, or lift it out with tongs, and drain off and reserve the marinade. If necessary, allow the food to come to room temperature before cooking.

6 Use the marinade for basting or brushing the food during cooking.

Cook's Tip
The amount of marinade you will need depends on the amount of food. As a rough guide, about 150ml/¼ pint/⅔ cup is enough for about 500g/1¼ lb of food.

BASIC BARBECUE MARINADE
This can be used for meat or fish.

1 garlic clove, crushed
45ml/3 tbsp sunflower or olive oil
45ml/3 tbsp dry sherry
15ml/1 tbsp Worcestershire sauce
15ml/1 tbsp dark soy sauce
freshly ground black pepper

RED WINE MARINADE
This is good with red meats and game.

150ml/¼ pint/⅔ cup dry red wine
15ml/1 tbsp olive oil
15ml/1 tbsp red wine vinegar
2 garlic cloves, crushed
2 dried bay leaves, crumbled
freshly ground black pepper

BELOW: *Marinating foods before cooking adds to the flavour and ensures the food is kept tender and moist.*

Starters & Snacks

SKEWERED LAMB WITH RED ONION SALSA

*A simple salsa makes a refreshing accompaniment to this summery dish – make sure you use a
mild-flavoured red onion that is fresh and crisp, and a tomato that is ripe and full of flavour.*

INGREDIENTS

225g/8oz lean lamb, cubed
2.5ml/½ tsp ground cumin
5ml/1 tsp ground paprika
15ml/1 tbsp olive oil
salt and freshly ground black
pepper

FOR THE SALSA
1 red onion, very thinly sliced
1 large tomato, seeded and
chopped
15ml/1 tbsp red wine vinegar
3–4 fresh basil or mint leaves,
roughly torn
small mint leaves, to garnish

SERVES 4

1 Place the lamb in a large bowl with the cumin, paprika and olive oil and season with plenty of salt and freshly ground black pepper. Toss well. Cover the bowl with clear film and leave in a cool place for several hours, or in the fridge overnight, so that the lamb fully absorbs the spicy flavours.

2 Spear the lamb cubes on four small skewers. If using wooden skewers, soak them first in cold water for at least 30 minutes to prevent them burning when placed on the barbecue.

3 To make the salsa, put the sliced onion, tomato, red wine vinegar and torn fresh basil or mint leaves in a small bowl and stir together until thoroughly blended. Season to taste with salt and garnish with mint.

4 Cook the skewered lamb on a hot barbecue, or under a hot grill, for about 5–10 minutes, turning the skewers frequently, until the lamb is well browned but still slightly pink in the centre. Serve hot, with the salsa.

HERB POLENTA

. ∘ .

Golden polenta with fresh summer herbs makes an appetizing starter or light snack, served with barbecued tomatoes.

INGREDIENTS

750ml/1¼ pints/3 cups stock or water
5ml/1 tsp salt
175g/6oz/1 cup polenta
25g/1oz/2 tbsp butter
75ml/5 tbsp mixed chopped fresh parsley, chives and basil, plus extra to garnish
olive oil for brushing
4 large plum or beef tomatoes, halved
salt and freshly ground black pepper

SERVES 4

3 Remove from the heat and stir in the butter, chopped herbs and pepper.

4 Lightly grease a wide tin or dish and tip the polenta into it, spreading it evenly. Leave until cool and set.

1 Prepare the polenta in advance: place the stock or water in a saucepan, with the salt, and bring to the boil. Reduce the heat and stir in the polenta.

2 Stir constantly over a moderate heat for 5 minutes, until the polenta begins to thicken and come away from the sides of the saucepan.

5 Turn out the polenta and cut into squares or stamp out rounds with a large biscuit cutter. Brush with olive oil. Lightly brush the tomatoes with oil and sprinkle with salt and pepper. Cook the tomatoes and polenta on a medium-hot barbecue for about 5 minutes, turning once. Serve garnished with fresh herbs.

Cook's Tip

Try using fresh basil or fresh chives alone, for a distinctive flavour.

BRIE PARCELS WITH ALMONDS

• • •

*Creamy French Brie makes a sophisticated starter or light meal, wrapped in
vine leaves and served hot with chunks of crusty bread.*

2 Cut the Brie into four chunks and place each chunk on a vine leaf.

3 Mix together the chives, ground almonds, peppercorns and olive oil, and place a spoonful on top of each piece of cheese. Sprinkle with flaked almonds.

4 Fold the vine leaves over tightly to enclose the cheese completely. Brush the parcels with olive oil and cook on a hot barbecue for about 3–4 minutes, until the cheese is hot and melting. Serve immediately.

INGREDIENTS

*4 large vine leaves, preserved in
brine
200g/7oz piece Brie cheese
30ml/2 tbsp chopped fresh chives
30ml/2 tbsp ground almonds
5ml/1 tsp crushed black
peppercorns
15ml/1 tbsp olive oil
flaked almonds*

SERVES **4**

1 Rinse the vine leaves thoroughly under cold running water and dry them well. Spread the leaves out on a clean work surface or chopping board.

SALMON WITH SPICY PESTO

· · ∘

*This is a great way to bone salmon steaks to give a solid piece of fish. The pesto uses
sunflower kernels and chilli as its flavouring, rather than the classic basil and pine nuts.*

INGREDIENTS
4 salmon steaks, about
225g/8oz each
30ml/2 tbsp sunflower oil
finely grated rind and juice
of 1 lime
salt and freshly ground
black pepper

FOR THE PESTO
6 mild fresh red chillies
2 garlic cloves
30ml/2 tbsp sunflower or
pumpkin seeds
juice and finely grated rind
of 1 lime
75ml/5 tbsp olive oil

SERVES 4

1 Insert a very sharp knife close to
the top of the bone. Working closely
to the bone, cut your way to the end
of the steak to release one side. Repeat
with the other side. Pull out any extra
visible bones with a pair of tweezers.

2 Sprinkle salt on the work surface
and take hold of the end of the salmon
piece, skin-side down. Insert the knife
between the skin and the flesh and,
working away from you, remove the
skin, keeping the knife as close to it as
possible. Repeat for each piece of fish.

3 Curl each piece of fish into a
round, with the thinner end wrapped
around the fatter end. Secure the shape
tightly with a length of string.

4 Rub the sunflower oil into the
boneless fish rounds. Put the salmon
into a large bowl or dish and add the
lime juice and rind and the salt and
pepper. Allow the salmon to marinate
in the fridge for up to 2 hours.

5 For the pesto, de-seed the chillies
and place with the garlic cloves,
sunflower or pumpkin seeds, lime juice,
rind and seasoning in a food processor.
Process until well mixed. Pour the olive
oil gradually over the moving blades
until the sauce has thickened and
emulsified. Drain the salmon from its
marinade. Cook the fish steaks on a
medium barbecue for 5 minutes each
side and serve with the spicy pesto.

SPICY MEATBALLS

These meatballs are delicious served piping hot with chilli sauce. Keep the sauce on the side so that everyone can add as much heat as they like.

2 Add the minced beef, shallots, garlic, breadcrumbs, beaten egg and parsley, with plenty of salt and pepper. Mix well, then use your hands to shape the mixture into 18 small balls.

3 Brush the meatballs with olive oil and cook on a medium barbecue, or fry them in a large pan, for about 10–15 minutes, turning regularly until evenly browned and cooked through.

INGREDIENTS

115g/4oz fresh spicy sausages
115g/4oz minced beef
2 shallots, finely chopped
2 garlic cloves, finely chopped
75g/3oz/1½ cups fresh white
breadcrumbs
1 egg, beaten
30ml/2 tbsp chopped fresh parsley,
plus extra to garnish
15ml/1 tbsp olive oil
salt and freshly ground black
pepper
Tabasco or other hot chilli sauce,
to serve

SERVES 6

1 Use your hands to remove the skins from the spicy sausages, placing the sausagemeat in a mixing bowl and breaking it up with a fork.

4 Transfer the meatballs to a warm dish and sprinkle with chopped fresh parsley. Serve with chilli sauce.

POLPETTES WITH MOZZARELLA AND TOMATO

*These Italian-style meatballs are made with beef and topped with creamy melted
mozzarella and savoury anchovies.*

INGREDIENTS

*½ slice white bread, crusts
removed*
45ml/3 tbsp milk
675g/1½ lb minced beef
1 egg, beaten
50g/2oz/⅔ cup dry breadcrumbs
olive oil for brushing
*2 beefsteak or other large
tomatoes, sliced*
15ml/1 tbsp chopped fresh oregano
*1 mozzarella cheese, cut into
6 slices*
*6 drained, canned anchovy fillets,
cut in half lengthways*
*salt and freshly ground black
pepper*

SERVES 6

1 Put the bread and milk into a small
saucepan and heat very gently, until the
bread absorbs all the milk. Mash it to a
pulp and set aside to cool.

2 Put the minced beef into a bowl
with the bread mixture and the egg and
season with plenty of salt and freshly
ground black pepper. Mix well, then
shape the mixture into six patties, using
your hands. Sprinkle the breadcrumbs
on to a plate and dredge the patties,
coating them thoroughly.

3 Brush the polpettes with olive oil
and cook them on a hot barbecue for
2–3 minutes on one side, until brown.
Turn them over.

4 Without removing the polpettes
from the barbecue, lay a slice of tomato
on top of each polpette, sprinkle with
chopped oregano and season with salt
and pepper. Place a mozzarella slice on
top and arrange two strips of anchovy
in a cross over the cheese.

5 Cook for a further 4–5 minutes
until the polpettes are cooked through
and the mozzarella has melted.

FIVE-SPICE RIB-STICKERS

• • •

*Choose the meatiest spare ribs you can find, to make these a real success, and
remember to keep a supply of paper napkins within easy reach.*

2 Mix together all the remaining
ingredients, except the spring onions,
and pour over the ribs. Toss well to
coat evenly. Cover the bowl and leave
to marinate in the fridge overnight.

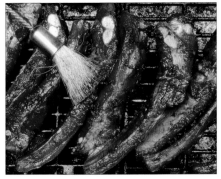

3 Cook the ribs on a medium-hot
barbecue, turning frequently, for about
30–40 minutes. Brush occasionally
with the remaining marinade.

INGREDIENTS

*1kg/2¼lb Chinese-style pork
spare ribs
10ml/2 tsp Chinese five-spice
powder
2 garlic cloves, crushed
15ml/1 tbsp grated fresh
root ginger
2.5ml/½ tsp chilli sauce
60ml/4 tbsp dark soy sauce
45ml/3 tbsp dark muscovado sugar
15ml/1 tbsp sunflower oil
4 spring onions*

SERVES 4

1 If the spare ribs are still attached
to each other, cut between them to
separate them (or you could ask your
butcher to do this when you buy them).
Place the spare ribs in a large bowl.

4 While the ribs are cooking, finely
slice the spring onions. Scatter them
over the ribs and serve immediately.

CHICKEN WINGS TERIYAKI STYLE

• • •

This oriental glaze is very simple to prepare and adds a unique flavour to the meat. The glaze can be used with any cut of chicken or with fish.

INGREDIENTS

1 garlic clove, crushed
45ml/3 tbsp soy sauce
30ml/2 tbsp dry sherry
10ml/2 tsp clear honey
10ml/2 tsp grated fresh root ginger
5ml/1 tsp sesame oil
12 chicken wings
15ml/1 tbsp sesame seeds, toasted

SERVES 4

1 Place the garlic, soy sauce, sherry, honey, grated ginger and sesame oil in a large bowl and beat with a fork, to mix the ingredients together evenly.

2 Add the chicken wings and toss thoroughly, to coat in the marinade. Cover the bowl with clear film and chill for about 30 minutes, or longer.

3 Cook the chicken wings on a fairly hot barbecue for about 20–25 minutes, turning occasionally and basting with the remaining marinade.

4 Sprinkle the chicken wings with sesame seeds. Serve the wings on their own as a starter or side dish, or with a crisp green salad.

MEAT

~

VEAL CHOPS WITH BASIL BUTTER

*Veal chops from the loin are an expensive cut and are best cooked quickly and simply.
The flavour of basil goes well with veal, but other herbs can be used instead if you prefer.*

INGREDIENTS
*25g/1oz/2 tbsp butter, softened
15ml/1 tbsp Dijon mustard
15ml/1 tbsp chopped fresh basil
olive oil, for brushing
2 veal loin chops, 2.5cm/1in thick,
about 225g/8oz each
salt and freshly ground black
pepper
fresh basil sprigs, to garnish*

SERVES 2

1 To make the basil butter, cream the softened butter with the Dijon mustard and chopped fresh basil in a large mixing bowl, then season with plenty of freshly ground black pepper.

2 Brush both sides of each chop with olive oil and season with a little salt.

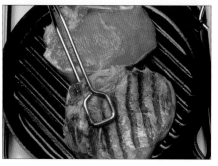

3 Cook the chops on a hot barbecue for 7–10 minutes, basting with oil and turning once, until done to your liking. (Medium-rare meat will still be slightly soft when pressed, medium meat will be springy and well-done firm.) Top each chop with half the basil butter and serve at once, garnished with basil.

MIXED GRILL SKEWERS WITH HORSERADISH SAUCE

. . .

This hearty selection of meats, cooked on a skewer and drizzled with horseradish sauce, makes a popular main course. Keep all the pieces of meat about the same thickness so they cook evenly.

INGREDIENTS

4 small lamb noisettes, each
about 2.5cm/1in thick
4 lamb's kidneys
4 streaky bacon rashers
8 cherry tomatoes
8 chipolata sausages
12–16 bay leaves
salt and freshly ground black
pepper

FOR THE HORSERADISH SAUCE
30ml/2 tbsp horseradish relish
45ml/3 tbsp melted butter

SERVES 4

3 Thread the lamb noisettes, bacon-wrapped kidneys and cherry tomatoes, chipolatas and bay leaves on to four long metal skewers. Set aside while you prepare the sauce.

4 Mix the horseradish relish with the melted butter in a small bowl and stir until thoroughly mixed.

5 Brush a little of the horseradish sauce over the meat and sprinkle with salt and freshly ground black pepper.

6 Cook the skewers on a medium barbecue for 12 minutes, turning occasionally, until the meat is golden brown and thoroughly cooked. Serve hot, drizzled with the remaining sauce.

1 Trim any excess fat from the lamb noisettes with a sharp knife. Halve the kidneys and remove the cores, using kitchen scissors.

2 Cut each bacon rasher in half and wrap around the tomatoes or kidneys.

SAUSAGES WITH PRUNES AND BACON

. . .

Sausages are a perennial barbecue favourite and this is a delicious way to ring the changes.
Serve with crusty French bread or warmed ciabatta.

2 Spread the cut surface with the mustard and then place three prunes in each sausage, pressing them in firmly.

3 Stretch the bacon rashers out thinly, using the back of a palette knife.

4 Wrap one bacon rasher tightly around each of the sausages, to hold them in shape. Cook over a hot barbecue for 15–18 minutes, turning occasionally, until evenly browned and thoroughly cooked. Serve at once, with lots of fresh crusty bread and the additional mustard.

INGREDIENTS

8 large, meaty sausages, such as
Toulouse or other good-quality
pork sausages
30ml/2 tbsp Dijon mustard, plus
extra to serve
24 ready-to-eat prunes
8 smoked streaky
bacon rashers

SERVES 4

1 Use a sharp knife to cut a long slit down the length of each sausage, about three-quarters of the way through.

SHISH KEBAB

∘ ∘ ∘

Many different kinds of kebab are eaten throughout the Middle East, and they are almost always cooked over an open wood or charcoal fire.

INGREDIENTS
450g/1lb boned leg of lamb, cubed
1 large green pepper, seeded and cut into squares
1 large yellow pepper, seeded and cut into squares
8 baby onions, halved
225g/8oz button mushrooms
4 tomatoes, halved
15ml/1 tbsp melted butter
bulgur wheat, to serve

FOR THE MARINADE
45ml/3 tbsp olive oil
juice of 1 lemon
2 garlic cloves, crushed
1 large onion, grated
15ml/1 tbsp fresh oregano
salt and freshly ground black pepper

SERVES 4

1 First make the marinade: blend together the olive oil, lemon juice, crushed garlic, onion, fresh oregano and seasoning. Place the meat in a shallow dish and pour over the marinade. Cover with clear film and leave to marinate for several hours, or overnight, in the fridge.

2 Thread the lamb on to metal skewers, alternating with pieces of pepper, onions and mushrooms. Thread the tomatoes on to separate skewers.

3 Cook the kebabs and tomatoes on a hot barbecue for 10 minutes, turning occasionally and basting with butter. Serve with bulgur wheat.

29

BACON KOFTA KEBABS AND SALAD

. . .

*Kofta kebabs can be made with any type of minced meat, but bacon is very successful,
if you have a food processor.*

INGREDIENTS

250g/9oz lean streaky bacon
rashers, roughly chopped
1 small onion, roughly chopped
1 celery stick, roughly chopped
75ml/5 tbsp fresh wholemeal
breadcrumbs
45ml/3 tbsp chopped fresh thyme
30ml/2 tbsp Worcestershire sauce
1 egg, beaten
salt and freshly ground black
pepper
olive oil, for brushing

FOR THE SALAD
115g/4oz/³⁄₄ cup bulgur wheat
60ml/4 tbsp toasted sunflower
seeds
15ml/1 tbsp olive oil
salt and freshly ground black
pepper
handful celery leaves, chopped

SERVES 4

1 Place the bacon, onion, celery and breadcrumbs in a food processor and process until chopped. Add the thyme, Worcestershire sauce and seasoning. Bind to a firm mixture with the egg.

2 Divide the mixture into eight equal portions and use your hands to shape them around eight bamboo skewers.

3 For the salad, place the bulgur wheat in a bowl and pour over boiling water to cover. Leave to stand for 30 minutes, until the grains are tender.

4 Drain well, then stir in the sunflower seeds, olive oil, salt and pepper. Stir in the celery leaves.

5 Cook the kofta skewers over a medium-hot barbecue for 8–10 minutes, turning occasionally, until golden brown. Serve with the salad.

PEPPERED STEAKS IN BEER AND GARLIC

The robust flavours of this dish will satisfy the heartiest appetites.
Serve the steaks with jacket potatoes and a crisp mixed salad.

2 Remove the steaks from the dish and reserve the marinade. Sprinkle the peppercorns over the steaks and press them into the surface.

3 Cook the steaks on a hot barbecue, basting them occasionally with the reserved marinade during cooking. (Take care when basting, as the alcohol will tend to flare up: spoon or brush on just a small amount at a time.)

INGREDIENTS

4 beef sirloin or rump steaks,
about 175g/6oz each
2 garlic cloves, crushed
120ml/4fl oz/¹/₂ cup brown
ale or stout
30ml/2 tbsp dark muscovado sugar
30ml/2 tbsp Worcestershire sauce
15ml/1 tbsp corn oil
15ml/1 tbsp crushed black
peppercorns

SERVES 4

1 Place the steaks in a dish and add the garlic, ale or stout, sugar, Worcestershire sauce and oil. Turn to coat evenly, then leave to marinate in the fridge for 2–3 hours or overnight.

4 Turn the steaks once during cooking, and cook them for about 3–6 minutes on each side, depending on how rare you like them.

SIRLOIN STEAKS WITH BLOODY MARY SAUCE

This cocktail of ingredients is just as delicious as the drink that inspired it, and as the alcohol evaporates in cooking you need not worry about a hangover.

INGREDIENTS

4 sirloin steaks, about 225g/8oz each

FOR THE MARINADE
30ml/2 tbsp dark soy sauce
60ml/4 tbsp balsamic vinegar
30ml/2 tbsp olive oil

FOR THE BLOODY MARY SAUCE
1kg/2¼lb very ripe tomatoes, peeled and chopped
tomato purée, if required
50g/2oz/½ cup chopped onions
2 spring onions
5ml/1 tsp chopped fresh coriander
5ml/1 tsp ground cumin
5ml/1 tsp salt
15ml/1 tbsp fresh lime juice
120ml/4fl oz/½ cup beef consommé
60ml/4 tbsp vodka
15ml/1 tbsp Worcestershire sauce

SERVES 4

1 Lay the steaks in a shallow dish. Mix the marinade ingredients together, pour over the steaks and leave to marinate in the fridge for at least 2 hours, turning once or twice.

2 Place all the sauce ingredients in a food processor and blend to a fairly smooth texture. If the tomatoes are not quite ripe, add a little tomato purée. Put in a saucepan, bring to the boil and simmer for about 5 minutes.

3 Remove the steaks from the dish and discard the marinade. Cook the steaks on a medium-hot barbecue for about 3–6 minutes each side, depending on how rare you like them, turning once during cooking. Serve the steaks with the Bloody Mary sauce.

33

STILTON BURGERS

*A variation on the traditional burger, this tasty recipe contains a delicious surprise:
a creamy filling of lightly melted Stilton cheese.*

INGREDIENTS

450g/1lb/4 cups minced beef
1 onion, chopped
1 celery stick, chopped
5ml/1 tsp dried mixed herbs
5ml/1 tsp prepared mustard
*50g/2oz/1/2 cup crumbled Stilton
cheese*
4 burger buns
*salt and freshly ground black
pepper*

SERVES 4

1 Mix the minced beef with the chopped onion, celery, mixed herbs and mustard. Season well with salt and pepper, and bring together with your hands to form a firm mixture.

2 Divide the mixture into eight equal portions. Shape four portions into rounds and flatten each one slightly. Place a little of the crumbled cheese in the centre of each round.

3 Shape and flatten the remaining four portions and place on top. Use your hands to mould the rounds together, encasing the crumbled cheese, and shaping them into four burgers.

4 Cook on a medium barbecue for about 10 minutes or until cooked through, turning once. Split the burger buns and place a burger inside each. Serve with salad and mustard pickle.

SPICED BEEF SATAY

Tender strips of steak threaded on skewers and spiced with the characteristic flavours of Indonesia are popular with everyone.

INGREDIENTS

450g/1lb rump steak, cut in
1cm/½ in strips
5ml/1 tsp coriander seeds, dry-fried
and ground
2.5ml/½ tsp cumin seeds, dry-fried
and ground
5ml/1 tsp tamarind pulp
1 small onion
2 garlic cloves
15ml/1 tbsp brown sugar
15ml/1 tbsp dark soy sauce
salt

TO SERVE
cucumber chunks
lemon or lime wedges
Sambal Kecap

MAKES 18 SKEWERS

1 Mix the meat and spices in a large non-metallic bowl. Soak the tamarind pulp in 75ml/3fl oz/⅓ cup water.

2 Strain the tamarind and reserve the juice. Put the onion, garlic, tamarind juice, sugar and soy sauce in a food processor and blend well.

3 Pour the marinade over the meat and spices in the bowl and toss well together. Leave for at least 1 hour.

4 Meanwhile, soak some bamboo skewers in water to prevent them from burning while cooking. Thread 5 or 6 pieces of meat on to each skewer and sprinkle with salt. Cook on a medium-hot barbecue, turning the skewers frequently and basting with the marinade, until the meat is tender.

5 Serve with cucumber chunks and wedges of lemon or lime for squeezing over the meat. Sambal Kecap makes a traditional accompaniment.

SAMBAL KECAP
Mix 1 fresh red chilli, seeded and finely chopped, 2 crushed garlic cloves and 60ml/4 tbsp dark soy sauce with 20ml/4 tsp lemon juice and 30ml/2 tbsp hot water in a bowl. Leave to stand for 30 minutes before serving.

LAMB STEAKS MARINATED IN MINT AND SHERRY

*The marinade in this recipe is extremely quick to prepare, and is the key
to its success: the sherry imparts a wonderful tang to the meat.*

INGREDIENTS
*6 large lamb steaks or
12 smaller chops*

FOR THE MARINADE
*30ml/2 tbsp chopped fresh mint
leaves
15ml/1 tbsp black peppercorns
1 medium onion, chopped
120ml/4fl oz/1/2 cup sherry
60ml/4 tbsp extra virgin olive oil
2 garlic cloves*

SERVES 6

1 Blend the mint leaves and peppercorns in a food processor until finely chopped. Add the onion and process again until smooth. Add the rest of the marinade ingredients and process until completely mixed. The marinade should be a thick consistency.

2 Add the marinade to the steaks or chops and cover with clear film. Leave in the fridge to marinate overnight.

3 Cook the steaks on a medium barbecue for 10–15 minutes, basting occasionally with the marinade.

SKEWERED LAMB WITH CORIANDER YOGURT

∘ ∘ ∘

These Turkish kebabs are traditionally made with lamb, but lean beef or pork work equally well.
You can alternate pieces of pepper, lemon or onions with the meat for extra flavour and colour.

INGREDIENTS
900g/2lb lean boneless lamb
1 large onion, grated
3 bay leaves
5 thyme or rosemary sprigs
grated rind and juice of 1 lemon
2.5ml/1/2 tsp caster sugar
75ml/3fl oz/1/3 cup olive oil
salt and freshly ground black
pepper
sprigs of fresh rosemary, to garnish
barbecued lemon wedges, to serve

FOR THE CORIANDER YOGURT
150ml/1/4 pint/2/3 cup thick natural
yogurt
15ml/1 tbsp chopped fresh mint
15ml/1 tbsp chopped fresh
coriander
10ml/2 tsp grated onion

SERVES 4

1 To make the coriander yogurt, mix together the natural yogurt, chopped fresh mint, chopped fresh coriander and grated onion. Transfer the yogurt to a serving bowl.

2 To make the kebabs, cut the lamb into 2.5cm/1in cubes and put in a bowl. Mix together the onion, herbs, lemon rind and juice, sugar and oil, then season to taste.

3 Pour the marinade over the meat in the bowl and stir to ensure the meat is thoroughly covered. Cover with clear film and leave to marinate in the fridge for several hours or overnight.

4 Drain the meat and thread on to metal skewers. Cook on a hot barbecue for about 10 minutes. Garnish with rosemary and barbecued lemon wedges and serve with the coriander yogurt.

LAMB BURGERS WITH REDCURRANT CHUTNEY

These rather special burgers take a little extra time to prepare but are well worth it.
The redcurrant chutney is the perfect complement to the minty lamb taste.

INGREDIENTS

500g/1¼ lb minced lean lamb
1 small onion, finely chopped
30ml/2 tbsp finely chopped
fresh mint
30ml/2 tbsp finely chopped
fresh parsley
115g/4oz mozzarella cheese
30ml/2 tbsp oil, for basting
salt and freshly ground black
pepper

FOR THE REDCURRANT CHUTNEY
115g/4oz/1½ cups fresh or frozen
redcurrants
10ml/2 tsp clear honey
5ml/1 tsp balsamic vinegar
30ml/2 tbsp finely chopped mint

SERVES 4

1 In a large bowl, mix together the minced lamb, chopped onion, mint and parsley until evenly combined. Season well with plenty of salt and freshly ground black pepper.

Cook's Tip

If time is short, or if fresh redcurrants are not available, serve the burgers with ready-made redcurrant sauce.

2 Roughly divide the meat mixture into eight equal pieces and use your hands to press each of the pieces into flat rounds.

3 Cut the mozzarella cheese into four chunks. Place one chunk of cheese on half the lamb rounds. Top each with another round of meat mixture.

4 Press each of the two rounds of meat together firmly, making four flattish burger shapes. Use your fingers to blend the edges and seal in the cheese completely.

5 Place all the ingredients for the chutney in a bowl and mash them together with a fork. Season well with salt and freshly ground black pepper.

6 Brush the lamb burgers with olive oil and cook them over a moderately hot barbecue for about 15 minutes, turning once, until golden brown. Serve with the redcurrant chutney.

PORK AND PINEAPPLE SATAY

This variation on the classic satay has added pineapple, but keeps the traditional coconut and peanut sauce.

INGREDIENTS

500g/1¼ lb pork fillet
1 small onion, chopped
1 garlic clove, chopped
60ml/4 tbsp soy sauce
finely grated rind of ½ lemon
5ml/1 tsp ground cumin
5ml/1 tsp ground coriander
5ml/1 tsp ground turmeric
5ml/1 tsp dark muscovado sugar
225g/8oz can pineapple chunks, or
1 small fresh pineapple, peeled and
diced
salt and freshly ground black
pepper

FOR THE SATAY SAUCE
175ml/6fl oz/¾ cup coconut milk
115g/4oz/6 tbsp crunchy peanut
butter
1 garlic clove, crushed
10ml/2 tsp soy sauce
5ml/1 tsp dark muscovado sugar

SERVES 4

2 Place the onion, garlic, soy sauce, lemon rind, spices and sugar in a blender or food processor. Add two pieces of pineapple and process until the mixture is almost smooth.

3 Add the paste to the pork, tossing well to coat evenly. Thread the pieces of pork on to bamboo skewers, with the remaining pineapple pieces.

4 To make the sauce, pour the coconut milk into a small saucepan and stir in the peanut butter. Stir in the remaining sauce ingredients and heat gently over the barbecue, stirring until smooth and hot. Cover and keep warm on the edge of the barbecue.

5 Cook the pork and pineapple skewers on a medium-hot barbecue for 10–12 minutes, turning occasionally, until golden brown and thoroughly cooked. Serve with the satay sauce.

1 Using a sharp kitchen knife, trim any fat from the pork fillet and cut it in 2.5cm/1in cubes. Place the meat in a large mixing bowl and set aside.

Cook's Tip
If you cannot buy coconut milk, use creamed coconut in a block. Dissolve a 50g/2oz piece in 150ml/¼ pint/⅔ cup boiling water and use as above.

INGREDIENTS

radish
½ cucu
Chi

For
50g/2oz r

2 shallots

2 ga
2 sma
5cm/
15ml/
30ml
15ml

15ml/1

1 P
Gas 6
45ml
onion
softer
heat
olives
fresh
taste

50
4
8
2

15

1 Using
the chicken
to the bon
and discar

2 To ma
cashew or
processor
grind unti

2 I
and
any
do s
piece
thick

CITRUS KEBABS

° ° °

Serve these succulent barbecued chicken kebabs on a bed of lettuce leaves, garnished with sprigs of fresh mint and orange and lemon slices.

INGREDIENTS

4 chicken breasts, skinned and
boned
fresh mint sprigs, to garnish
orange, lemon or lime slices, to
garnish

FOR THE MARINADE
finely grated rind and juice of
1/2 orange
finely grated rind and juice of
1/2 lemon or lime
30ml/2 tbsp olive oil
30ml/2 tbsp clear honey
30ml/2 tbsp chopped fresh mint
1.5ml/1/4 tsp ground cumin
salt and freshly ground black
pepper

SERVES 4

1 Use a heavy knife to cut the chicken into 2.5cm/1in cubes.

2 Mix the marinade ingredients together in a large mixing bowl, add the chicken and cover with clear film. Leave to marinate for at least 2 hours, or overnight in the fridge.

3 Thread the chicken on to metal skewers and cook on a medium barbecue for 10 minutes, basting with the marinade and turning frequently. Garnish with mint and citrus slices.

SWEET AND SOUR KEBABS

• • •

This marinade contains sugar and will burn very easily, so cook the kebabs slowly and turn them often. Serve these kebabs with Harlequin Rice.

INGREDIENTS

2 chicken breasts, skinned and boned
8 pickling onions or 2 medium onions
4 rindless streaky bacon rashers
3 firm bananas
1 red pepper, diced

FOR THE MARINADE
30ml/2 tbsp soft brown sugar
15ml/1 tbsp Worcestershire sauce
30ml/2 tbsp lemon juice
salt and freshly ground black pepper

FOR THE HARLEQUIN RICE
30ml/2 tbsp olive oil
1 small red pepper, diced
225g/8oz/generous 1 cup cooked rice
115g/4oz/1 cup cooked peas

SERVES 4

1 Mix together the marinade ingredients. Cut each chicken breast into four pieces, add to the marinade, cover and leave for at least 4 hours, or preferably overnight in the fridge.

3 Cut each rasher of bacon in half with a sharp knife. Peel the bananas and cut each one into three pieces. Wrap half a bacon rasher around each of the banana pieces.

5 Cook on a low barbecue for about 15 minutes, turning and basting frequently with the marinade.

6 Meanwhile, heat the oil in a frying pan and stir-fry the diced pepper briefly. Add the rice and peas and stir until heated through. Serve the Harlequin Rice with the kebabs.

2 Peel the pickling onions, blanch them in boiling water for 5 minutes and drain. If using medium onions, quarter them after blanching.

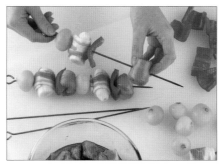

4 Thread the bacon and bananas on to metal skewers with the chicken pieces, onions and pepper pieces. Brush generously with the marinade.

BLACKENED CAJUN CHICKEN AND CORN

This is a classic American Deep-South method of cooking in a spiced coating, which can be used for poultry, meat or fish. The coating should begin to char and blacken slightly at the edges.

INGREDIENTS

8 chicken joints (drumsticks, thighs or wings)
2 whole corn cobs
10ml/2 tsp garlic salt
10ml/2 tsp ground black pepper
7.5ml/1½ tsp ground cumin
7.5ml/1½ tsp paprika
5ml/1 tsp cayenne pepper
45ml/3 tbsp melted butter
chopped parsley, to garnish

SERVES 4

1 Trim any excess fat from the chicken, but leave the skin in place. Slash the thickest parts with a knife, to allow the flavours to penetrate the meat as much as possible.

2 Pull the husks and silks off the corn cobs, then rinse them under cold running water and pat them dry with kitchen paper. Cut the cobs into thick slices, using a heavy kitchen knife.

3 Mix together all the spices. Brush the chicken and corn with the melted butter and sprinkle the spices over them. Toss well to coat evenly.

4 Cook the chicken pieces on a medium-hot barbecue for about 25 minutes, turning occasionally. Add the corn after 15 minutes, and grill, turning often, until golden brown. Serve garnished with chopped parsley.

CHICKEN WITH HERB AND RICOTTA STUFFING

* * *

*These little chicken drumsticks are full of flavour and the stuffing and bacon help to
keep them moist and tender.*

INGREDIENTS

60ml/4 tbsp ricotta cheese
1 garlic clove, crushed
*45ml/3 tbsp mixed chopped fresh
herbs, such as chives, flat-leaf
parsley and mint*
*30ml/2 tbsp fresh brown
breadcrumbs*
8 chicken drumsticks
8 smoked streaky bacon rashers
5ml/1 tsp whole-grain mustard
15ml/1 tbsp sunflower oil
*salt and freshly ground black
pepper*

SERVES 4

1 Mix together the ricotta, garlic, herbs and breadcrumbs. Season well with plenty of salt and pepper.

2 Carefully loosen the skin from each drumstick and spoon a little of the herb stuffing under each, smoothing the skin back over firmly.

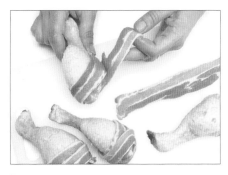

3 Wrap a bacon rasher tightly around the wide end of each drumstick, to hold the skin in place over the stuffing during the cooking time.

4 Mix together the mustard and oil and brush them over the chicken. Cook on a medium-hot barbecue for about 25 minutes, turning occasionally.

BABY CHICKENS WITH LIME AND CHILLI

∘ ∘ ∘

Poussins are small birds which are ideal for one to two portions. The best way to prepare them is spatchcocked – flattened out – to ensure more even cooking.

INGREDIENTS

4 poussins or Cornish hens, about
450g/1lb each
45ml/3 tbsp butter
30ml/2 tbsp sun-dried tomato
paste
finely grated rind of 1 lime
10ml/2 tsp chilli sauce
juice of ½ lime
lime wedges, to serve
fresh flat leaf parsley sprigs,
to garnish

SERVES 4

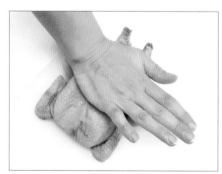

1 Place each poussin on a chopping board, breast-side upwards, and press down firmly with your hand, to break the breastbone.

2 Turn the poussin over and, with poultry shears or strong kitchen scissors, cut down either side of the backbone. Remove it and discard.

3 Turn the poussin breast-side up and flatten it gently. Lift the breast skin carefully and gently ease your fingertips underneath, to loosen it from the flesh.

4 Mix together the butter, sun-dried tomato paste, lime rind and chilli sauce in a small bowl. Spread about three-quarters of the mixture under the skin of the poussins, smoothing it evenly over the surface of the flesh.

5 To hold the poussins flat during cooking, thread two bamboo skewers through each bird, crossing at the centre. Each skewer should pass through a drumstick and then out through a wing on the other side.

6 Mix the reserved paste with the lime juice and brush it over the skin of the poussins. Cook on a medium-hot barbecue, turning occasionally, for 25–30 minutes, or until there is no trace of pink in the juices when the flesh is pierced. Garnish with lime wedges and fresh flat leaf parsley.

THAI GRILLED CHICKEN

· · ·

Thai grilled chicken is especially delicious when cooked on the barbecue.
Serve it on a bed of crisp salad with lime wedges to offset its richness.

INGREDIENTS

900g/2lb chicken drumsticks or
thighs
salt and freshly ground
black pepper
crisp lettuce leaves, to serve
1/2 cucumber, cut into strips,
to garnish
4 spring onions, trimmed,
to garnish
2 limes, quartered, to garnish

FOR THE MARINADE
5ml/1 tsp black peppercorns
2.5ml/1/2 tsp caraway or cumin
seeds
20ml/4 tsp sugar
10ml/2 tsp paprika
2cm/3/4in piece fresh root ginger,
chopped
3 garlic cloves, crushed
15g/1/2oz coriander, white root or
stem, finely chopped
45ml/3 tbsp vegetable oil

SERVES 4–6

1 Chop through the narrow end of each drumstick with a heavy knife. Score the chicken pieces deeply to allow the marinade to penetrate and arrange in a shallow bowl.

2 Grind the peppercorns, caraway or cumin seeds and sugar in a pestle and mortar or a food processor. Add the paprika, ginger, garlic, coriander and oil and grind to a paste.

3 Spread the marinade over the chicken and leave to marinate in the fridge for 6 hours. Cook the chicken on a medium barbecue for about 20 minutes, basting with the marinade and turning once. Season, arrange on a bed of lettuce and garnish before serving.

MEDITERRANEAN TURKEY SKEWERS

These attractive kebabs can be assembled in advance and left to marinate until you are ready to cook them. Barbecuing intensifies the Mediterranean flavours of the vegetables.

INGREDIENTS

2 medium courgettes
1 long thin aubergine
300g/11oz boneless turkey, cut into 5cm/2in cubes
12–16 pickling onions
1 red or yellow pepper, cut into 5cm/2in squares

FOR THE MARINADE
90ml/6 tbsp olive oil
45ml/3 tbsp fresh lemon juice
1 garlic clove, finely chopped
30ml/2 tbsp chopped fresh basil
salt and freshly ground black pepper

SERVES 4

3 Prepare the skewers by alternating the turkey, onions and pepper pieces. Lay the prepared skewers on a platter and sprinkle with the flavoured oil. Leave to marinate for 30 minutes.

4 Cook on a medium barbecue or under a grill for about 10 minutes, or until the turkey is cooked and the vegetables are tender, turning the skewers occasionally.

1 To make the marinade, mix the olive oil with the lemon juice, garlic and chopped fresh basil. Season well with plenty of salt and black pepper.

2 Slice the courgettes and aubergine lengthways into strips 5mm/¼ in thick. Cut them crossways about two-thirds down their length. Discard the shorter lengths. Wrap half the turkey pieces with the courgette slices and the other half with the aubergine slices.

QUAIL WITH A FIVE-SPICE MARINADE
. . .

Blending and grinding your own five-spice powder for this Vietnamese dish will give the freshest-tasting results. If you are short of time, buy a ready-mixed blend from the supermarket.

INGREDIENTS
6 quails, cleaned
2 spring onions, roughly chopped,
to garnish
mandarin orange or satsuma, to
garnish
banana leaves, to serve

FOR THE MARINADE
2 pieces star anise
10ml/2 tsp ground cinnamon
10ml/2 tsp fennel seeds
10ml/2 tsp Sichuan pepper
a pinch ground cloves
1 small onion, finely chopped
1 garlic clove, crushed
60ml/4 tbsp clear honey
30ml/2 tbsp dark soy sauce

SERVES 4–6

1 Remove the backbones from the quails by cutting down either side with a pair of strong kitchen scissors.

2 Flatten the birds with the palm of your hand and secure each bird using two bamboo skewers.

3 To make the marinade, place the five spices in a pestle and mortar or spice mill and grind into a fine powder. Add the chopped onion, garlic, clear honey and soy sauce, and combine until thoroughly mixed.

4 Arrange the quails on a flat dish and pour over the marinade. Cover with clear film and leave in the fridge for 8 hours or overnight for the flavours to mingle.

5 Cook the quails on a medium barbecue for 15–20 minutes until golden brown, basting occasionally with the marinade and turning once.

6 To garnish, remove the outer zest from the mandarin orange or satsuma, using a vegetable peeler. Shred the zest finely and combine with the chopped spring onions. Arrange the quails on a bed of banana leaves and garnish with the orange zest and spring onions.

Cook's Tip
If you prefer, or if quails are not available, you could use other poultry such as poussins as a substitute.

DUCK BREASTS WITH RED PLUMS

· · ·

The rich fruity sauce for this dish combines brandy and red plums with double cream and coriander. The sauce can be made in a pan on the barbecue while the duck is cooking.

INGREDIENTS

*4 duck breasts, about 175g/6oz
each, skinned
10ml/2 tsp crushed cinnamon stick
50g/2oz/¼ cup butter
15ml/1 tbsp plum brandy or
Cognac
250ml/8fl oz/1 cup chicken stock
250ml/8fl oz/1 cup double cream
6 fresh red plums, stoned and sliced
6 sprigs fresh coriander leaves, plus
extra to garnish
salt and freshly ground black
pepper*

SERVES 4

1 Score the duck breasts and sprinkle with salt. Press the crushed cinnamon on to both sides of the duck breasts. Brush with butter and cook on a medium barbecue for 15–20 minutes, turning once, until the duck is tender.

2 To make the sauce, melt half the remaining butter in a saucepan. Add the brandy or Cognac and set it alight. When the flames have died down, add the stock and cream and allow to simmer gently until reduced and thick. Add seasoning to taste.

3 In a saucepan, melt the other half of the butter and fry the plums and coriander just enough to cook the fruit through. Slice the duck breasts and pour some sauce around each one, then garnish with the plum slices and the chopped fresh coriander.

DUCK BREASTS WITH RED PEPPER JELLY GLAZE

*Sweet potatoes have pinkish skins and flesh varying from creamy white to deep orange.
Choose a long cylindrical tuber to make neat round slices for this Cajun dish.*

INGREDIENTS

*2 duck breasts
1 sweet potato, about 400g/14oz
30ml/2 tbsp red pepper jelly
15ml/1 tbsp sherry vinegar
50g/2oz/4 tbsp butter, melted
coarse sea salt and freshly ground
black pepper*

SERVES 2

4 Meanwhile, warm the red pepper jelly and sherry vinegar together in a bowl set over a saucepan of hot water, stirring to mix them as the jelly melts. Brush the skin of the duck with this jelly glaze and return to the barbecue, skin-side down, for a further 2–3 minutes to caramelize it.

5 Brush the sweet potato slices with melted butter and sprinkle with coarse sea salt. Cook on a hot barbecue for 8–10 minutes until soft, brushing with more butter and sprinkling with salt and pepper when you turn them. Serve the duck sliced with the sweet potatoes and accompany with a green salad.

1 Slash the skin of the duck breasts diagonally at 2.5cm/1in intervals and rub plenty of salt and pepper over the skin and into the cuts.

2 Scrub the sweet potato and cut into 1cm/½in slices, discarding the ends.

3 Cook the duck breasts on a medium barbecue, skin-side down, for 5 minutes. Turn and cook for a further 8–10 minutes, according to how pink you like your duck.

FISH & SEAFOOD

~

TIGER PRAWN SKEWERS WITH WALNUT PESTO

. . .

*This is an unusual starter or main course, which can be prepared in advance and kept
in the fridge until you're ready to cook it.*

INGREDIENTS

12–16 large, raw, shell-on tiger
prawns
50g/2oz/¹/₂ cup walnut pieces
60ml/4 tbsp chopped fresh flat-leaf
parsley
60ml/4 tbsp chopped fresh basil
2 garlic cloves, chopped
45ml/3 tbsp grated fresh Parmesan
cheese
30ml/2 tbsp extra virgin olive oil
30ml/2 tbsp walnut oil
salt and freshly ground black
pepper

SERVES 4

3 Add half the pesto to the prawns
in the bowl, toss them well, then cover
and chill in the fridge for a minimum
of 1 hour, or leave them overnight.

4 Thread the prawns on to skewers
and cook them on a hot barbecue for
3–4 minutes, turning once. Serve with
the remaining pesto and a green salad.

1 Peel the prawns, removing the head
but leaving the tail. De-vein and then
put the prawns in a large mixing bowl.

2 To make the pesto, place the
walnuts, parsley, basil, garlic, cheese
and oils in a food processor and
process until finely chopped. Season.

SWORDFISH KEBABS

. . .

*Swordfish has a firm meaty texture that makes it ideal for cooking on a barbecue.
Marinade the fish first to keep it moist.*

INGREDIENTS

*900g/2lb swordfish steaks
45ml/3 tbsp olive oil
juice of 1/2 lemon
1 garlic clove, crushed
5ml/1 tsp paprika
3 tomatoes, quartered
2 onions, cut into wedges
salt and freshly ground black
pepper
salad and pitta bread, to serve*

SERVES 4–6

1 Use a large kitchen knife to cut the swordfish steaks into large cubes. Arrange the cubes in a single layer in a large shallow dish.

2 Blend together the olive oil, lemon juice, garlic, paprika and seasoning in a bowl, and pour over the fish. Cover the dish loosely with clear film and leave to marinate in a cool place for up to 2 hours.

3 Thread the fish cubes on to metal skewers, alternating them with the pieces of tomato and onion wedges.

4 Cook the kebabs on a hot barbecue for about 5–10 minutes, basting frequently with the remaining marinade and turning occasionally. Serve with salad and pitta bread.

CALAMARI WITH TWO-TOMATO STUFFING

*Calamari, or baby squid, are quick to cook, but do turn and baste them often
and take care not to overcook them.*

INGREDIENTS

500g/1¼ lb baby squid, cleaned
1 garlic clove, crushed
3 plum tomatoes, skinned and
chopped
8 sun-dried tomatoes in oil,
drained and chopped
60ml/4 tbsp chopped fresh basil,
plus extra, to serve
60ml/4 tbsp fresh white
breadcrumbs
45ml/3 tbsp olive oil
15ml/1 tbsp red wine vinegar
salt and freshly ground black
pepper
lemon juice, to serve

SERVES 4

1 Remove the tentacles from the
squid and roughly chop them; leave
the main part of the squid whole.

2 Mix together the crushed garlic,
plum tomatoes, sun-dried tomatoes,
chopped fresh basil and breadcrumbs.
Stir in 15ml/1 tbsp of the olive oil and
the vinegar. Season well with plenty of
salt and freshly ground black pepper.
Soak some wooden cocktail sticks in
water for 10 minutes before use, to
prevent them burning on the barbecue.

3 Using a teaspoon, fill the squid
with the stuffing mixture. Secure the
open ends with the cocktail sticks to
hold the stuffing mixture in place.

4 Brush the squid with the remaining
olive oil and cook over a medium-hot
barbecue for 4–5 minutes, turning
often. Sprinkle with lemon juice and
extra chopped fresh basil to serve.

BARBECUED SCALLOPS WITH LIME BUTTER

• • •

*Fresh scallops are quick to cook and ideal for barbecues. This recipe combines them
simply with lime and fennel.*

INGREDIENTS

1 head fennel
2 limes
12 large scallops, cleaned
1 egg yolk
90ml/6 tbsp melted butter
olive oil for brushing
salt and freshly ground
black pepper

SERVES 4

3 Place the egg yolk and remaining lime rind and juice in a small bowl and whisk until pale and smooth.

5 Brush the fennel wedges with olive oil and cook them on a hot barbecue for 3–4 minutes, turning once.

1 Trim any feathery leaves from the fennel and reserve them. Slice the rest lengthways into thin wedges.

4 Gradually whisk in the melted butter and continue whisking until thick and smooth. Finely chop the reserved fennel leaves and stir them in, with seasoning to taste.

6 Add the scallops and cook for a further 3–4 minutes, turning once. Serve with the lime and fennel butter and the lime wedges.

2 Cut one lime into wedges. Finely grate the rind and squeeze the juice of the other lime and toss half the juice and rind on to the scallops. Season well with salt and fresh black pepper.

Cook's Tip
If the scallops are small, you may wish to thread them on to flat skewers to make turning them easier.

TROUT WITH BACON

· · ·

*The smoky, savoury flavour of crispy grilled bacon perfectly complements
the delicate flesh of the trout in this simple dish.*

INGREDIENTS

4 trout, cleaned and gutted
25g/1oz/1 tbsp plain flour
4 rashers smoked streaky bacon
30ml/2 tbsp olive oil
juice of 1/2 lemon
salt and freshly ground
black pepper

SERVES 4

1 Place the trout on a chopping board and pat dry with kitchen paper. Season the flour with the salt and freshly ground black pepper. Stretch the bacon rashers out thinly using the back of a heavy kitchen knife.

2 Roll the fish in the seasoned flour mixture and wrap tightly in the streaky bacon. Brush with olive oil and cook on a medium-hot barbecue for 10–15 minutes, turning once. Serve at once, with the lemon juice drizzled on top.

SARDINES WITH WARM HERB SALSA

Plain grilling is the very best way to cook fresh sardines. Served with this luscious herb salsa the only other essential item is fresh, crusty bread, to mop up the tasty juices.

INGREDIENTS

12–16 fresh sardines
oil for brushing
juice of 1 lemon

FOR THE SALSA
15ml/1 tbsp butter
4 spring onions, chopped
1 garlic clove, finely chopped
rind of 1 lemon
30ml/2 tbsp finely chopped fresh parsley
30ml/2 tbsp finely snipped fresh chives
30ml/2 tbsp finely chopped fresh basil
30ml/2 tbsp green olive paste
10ml/2 tsp balsamic vinegar
salt and freshly ground black pepper

SERVES 4

1 To clean the sardines, use a pair of small kitchen scissors to slit the fish along the belly and pull out the innards. Wipe the fish with kitchen paper and then arrange on a grill rack.

2 To make the salsa, melt the butter in a small pan and gently sauté the spring onions and garlic for about 2 minutes, shaking the pan occasionally, until softened but not browned.

3 Add the lemon rind and remaining salsa ingredients to the onions and garlic in the pan and keep warm on the edge of the barbecue, stirring occasionally. Do not allow to boil.

4 Brush the sardines lightly with oil and sprinkle with lemon juice, salt and pepper. Cook for about 2 minutes on each side, over a moderate heat. Serve with the warm salsa and crusty bread.

MONKFISH WITH PEPPERED CITRUS MARINADE

Monkfish is a firm, meaty fish that cooks well on the barbecue and keeps its shape.
Serve with a green salad.

INGREDIENTS

2 monkfish tails, about
350g/12oz each
1 lime
1 lemon
2 oranges
handful of fresh thyme sprigs
30ml/2 tbsp olive oil
15ml/1 tbsp mixed peppercorns,
roughly crushed
salt and freshly ground
black pepper

SERVES 4

2 Turn the fish and repeat on the other side, to remove the second fillet. Repeat on the second tail. (If you prefer, you can ask your fishmonger to do this for you.) Lay the four fillets out flat on a chopping board.

5 Squeeze the juice from the citrus fruits and mix it with the olive oil and more salt and pepper. Spoon over the fish. Cover with clear film and leave to marinate in the fridge for about 1 hour, turning occasionally and spooning the marinade over the fish.

1 Using a sharp kitchen knife, remove any skin from the monkfish tails. Cut carefully down one side of the backbone, sliding the knife between the bone and flesh, to remove the fillet on one side.

3 Cut two slices from each of the citrus fruits and arrange them over two of the fillets. Add a few sprigs of fresh thyme and sprinkle with plenty of salt and freshly ground black pepper. Finely grate the rind from the remaining fruit and sprinkle it over the fish.

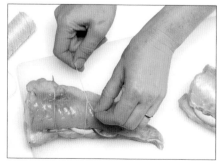

4 Lay the other two fillets on top and tie them firmly at intervals.

6 Drain the monkfish, reserving the marinade, and sprinkle with the crushed peppercorns. Cook on a medium-hot barbecue for 15–20 minutes, basting with the marinade and turning occasionally, until the fish is evenly cooked.

CHAR-GRILLED TUNA WITH FIERY PEPPER PUREE

Tuna is an oily fish that barbecues well and is meaty enough to combine successfully with strong flavours – even hot chilli, as in this red pepper purée, which is excellent served with crusty bread.

INGREDIENTS

4 tuna steaks, about 175g/6oz each
finely grated rind and juice of 1 lime
30ml/2 tbsp olive oil
salt and freshly ground black pepper
lime wedges, to serve

FOR THE PEPPER PURÉE
2 red peppers, halved
45ml/3 tbsp olive oil, plus extra for
brushing
1 small onion
2 garlic cloves, crushed
2 red chillies
1 slice white bread without crusts,
diced
salt

SERVES 4

2 To make the pepper purée, brush the pepper halves with a little olive oil and cook them, skin-side down, on a hot barbecue, until the skin is charred and blackened. Place the onion in its skin on the barbecue and cook until browned, turning it occasionally.

3 Leave the peppers and onion until cool enough to handle, then remove the skins, using a sharp kitchen knife.

4 Place the cooked peppers and onion with the garlic, chillies, bread and olive oil in a food processor. Process until smooth. Add salt to taste.

5 Drain the tuna steaks from the marinade and cook them on a hot barbecue for 8–10 minutes, turning once, until golden brown. Serve the steaks with the pepper purée and lime wedges, with crusty bread if liked.

1 Trim any skin from the tuna and place the steaks in a single layer in a wide dish. Sprinkle over the lime rind and juice, olive oil, salt and black pepper. Cover with clear film and chill in the fridge until required.

Cook's Tip

The pepper purée can be made in advance, cooking the peppers and onion under a hot grill; keep it in the fridge until you cook the fish.

GRILLED SEA BASS WITH CITRUS FRUIT

Sea bass is a beautiful fish with a soft, dense texture and a delicate flavour. In this recipe it is complemented by citrus fruits and fruity olive oil.

INGREDIENTS

1 small grapefruit
1 orange
1 lemon
1 sea bass, about 1.5kg/
3–3½ lb, cleaned and
scaled
6 fresh basil sprigs
45ml/3 tbsp olive oil
4–6 shallots, halved
60ml/4 tbsp dry white wine
15g/½ oz/1 tbsp butter
salt and freshly ground black
pepper
fresh dill, to garnish

SERVES 6

1 Using a vegetable peeler, remove the rind from the grapefruit, orange and lemon. Cut into thin julienne strips. Peel the pith from the fruits and, working over a bowl to catch the juices, cut out the segments from the grapefruit and the orange and set aside for the garnish. Slice the lemon thickly.

2 Season the cavity of the fish with salt and pepper and slash the flesh three times on each side. Reserving a few basil sprigs for the garnish, fill the cavity with the remaining basil, the lemon slices and half the julienne strips of citrus rind. Brush with olive oil and cook on a low–medium barbecue for about 20 minutes, basting occasionally and turning once.

3 Meanwhile, heat 15ml/1 tbsp olive oil in a pan and cook the shallots gently until soft. Add the wine and 30–45ml/2–3 tbsp of the fruit juice to the pan. Bring to the boil over a high heat, stirring. Stir in the remaining julienne strips of rind and boil for 2–3 minutes, then whisk in the butter.

4 When the fish is cooked, transfer it to a serving dish. Remove and discard the cavity stuffing. Spoon the shallots and sauce around the fish and garnish with fresh dill sprigs, the reserved basil and segments of grapefruit and orange.

SEA BREAM WITH ORANGE BUTTER SAUCE

Sea bream is a revelation to anyone unfamiliar with its creamy rich flavour.
The fish has a firm white flesh that goes well with this rich butter sauce, sharpened with orange.

INGREDIENTS

2 sea bream, about 350g/12oz
each, scaled and gutted
10ml/2 tsp Dijon mustard
5ml/1 tsp fennel seeds
30ml/2 tbsp olive oil
50g/2oz watercress
175g/6oz mixed lettuce leaves,
such as curly endive or frisée

FOR THE ORANGE BUTTER SAUCE
30ml/2 tbsp frozen orange juice
concentrate
175g/6oz/3/4 cup unsalted butter,
diced
salt and cayenne pepper

SERVES 2

1 Slash the sea bream four times on either side. Combine the mustard and fennel seeds, then spread over both sides of the fish. Brush with olive oil and cook on a medium-hot barbecue for 10–12 minutes, turning once.

2 Place the orange juice concentrate in a bowl and heat over a saucepan of simmering water. Remove the pan from the heat and gradually whisk in the butter until creamy. Season well.

3 Dress the watercress and lettuce leaves with the remaining olive oil, and arrange with the fish on two plates. Spoon the sauce over the fish and serve with jacket potatoes, if liked.

71

MACKEREL KEBABS WITH SWEET PEPPER SALAD

Mackerel is an excellent fish for barbecuing because its natural oils keep it moist and tasty. This recipe combines mackerel with peppers and tomatoes in a flavoursome summer salad.

INGREDIENTS

4 medium mackerel, about
225g/8oz each, filleted
2 small red onions, cut in wedges
30ml/2 tbsp chopped fresh
marjoram
60ml/4 tbsp dry white wine
45ml/3 tbsp olive oil
juice of 1 lime

FOR THE SALAD

1 red pepper
1 yellow pepper
1 small red onion
2 large plum tomatoes
15ml/1 tbsp chopped fresh
marjoram
10ml/2 tsp balsamic vinegar
salt and freshly ground black
pepper

SERVES 4

1 Thread each mackerel fillet on to a skewer, with an onion wedge on each end. Arrange the skewers in a dish.

2 Mix together the marjoram, wine, oil and lime juice and spoon over the mackerel. Cover and chill in the fridge for at least 30 minutes, turning once.

3 To make the salad, quarter and seed both peppers and halve the onion. Place the peppers and onion, skin-side down, with the whole tomatoes, on a hot barbecue and leave until the skins are blackened and charred.

4 Remove the vegetables from the barbecue and leave until they are cool enough to handle. Use a sharp knife to peel off and discard the skins.

5 Chop the vegetables roughly and put them in a bowl. Stir in the marjoram and balsamic vinegar and season to taste. Toss thoroughly.

6 Remove the kebabs from the fridge and cook on a hot barbecue for about 10–12 minutes, turning occasionally and basting with the marinade. Serve with the pepper salad.

Cook's Tip

Other oily fish can be used for this dish: try fillets or cubes of herring, rainbow trout or salmon, instead.

VEGETARIAN
&VEGETABLE
DISHES

~

VEGETABLE PARCELS WITH FLOWERY BUTTER

Nasturtium leaves and flowers are edible and have a distinctive peppery flavour.
They make a pretty addition to summer barbecue dishes.

INGREDIENTS

200g/7oz baby carrots
250g/9oz yellow patty-pan
squashes or yellow courgettes
115g/4oz baby sweetcorn
1 onion, thinly sliced
50g/2oz/4 tbsp butter, plus extra
for greasing
finely grated rind of ½ lemon
6 young nasturtium leaves
4–8 nasturtium flowers
salt and freshly ground
black pepper

SERVES 4

1 Trim the vegetables with a sharp knife, leaving them whole unless they are very large – if necessary, cut them into even-size pieces.

2 Divide the vegetables between four double-thickness squares of buttered baking foil and season well.

3 Mix the butter with the lemon rind in a small bowl. Roughly chop the nasturtium leaves and add them to the butter. Place a generous spoonful of the butter on each pile of vegetables in the squares of baking foil.

4 Fold over the foil and seal the edges to make a neat parcel. Cook on a medium-hot barbecue for 30 minutes until the vegetables are tender. Open the parcels and top each with one or two nasturtium flowers. Serve at once.

SUMMER VEGETABLES WITH YOGURT PESTO

• • •

Char-grilled vegetables make a meal on their own, or are delicious served as a Mediterranean-style accompaniment to grilled meats and fish.

INGREDIENTS

2 small aubergines
2 large courgettes
1 red pepper
1 yellow pepper
1 fennel bulb
1 red onion
olive oil, for brushing
salt and freshly ground black pepper

FOR THE YOGURT PESTO
150ml/1/4 pint/2/3 cup Greek-style yogurt
45ml/3 tbsp pesto

SERVES 4

1 Cut the aubergines into 1cm/1/2in slices. Sprinkle with salt and leave to drain for about 30 minutes. Rinse well in cold running water and pat dry.

2 Use a sharp kitchen knife to cut the courgettes in half lengthways. Cut the peppers in half, removing the seeds but leaving the stalks in place.

3 Slice the fennel bulb and the red onion into thick wedges, using a sharp kitchen knife.

4 Stir the yogurt and pesto lightly together in a bowl, to make a marbled sauce. Spoon the yogurt pesto into a serving bowl and set aside.

5 Arrange the vegetables on the hot barbecue, brush generously with olive oil and sprinkle with plenty of salt and freshly ground black pepper.

6 Cook the vegetables until golden brown and tender, turning occasionally. The aubergines and peppers will take 6–8 minutes to cook, the courgettes, onion and fennel 4–5 minutes. Serve the vegetables as soon as they are cooked, with the yogurt pesto.

Cook's Tip

Baby vegetables make excellent candidates for grilling whole, so look out for baby aubergines and peppers, in particular. There's no need to salt the aubergines if they're small.

BARBECUED GOAT'S CHEESE PIZZA

• • •

Pizzas cooked on the barbecue have a beautifully crisp and golden base. The combination of goat's cheese and red onion in this recipe makes for a flavoursome main course dish.

2 Brush the dough round with olive oil and place, oiled side down, on a medium barbecue. Cook for about 6–8 minutes until firm and golden underneath. Brush the uncooked side with olive oil and turn the pizza over.

3 Mix together the passata and red pesto and quickly spread over the cooked side of the pizza, to within about 1cm/½in of the edge. Arrange the onion, tomatoes and cheese on top and sprinkle with salt and pepper.

INGREDIENTS

150g/5oz packet pizza-base mix
olive oil, for brushing
150ml/¼ pint/⅔ cup passata
30ml/2 tbsp red pesto
1 small red onion, thinly sliced
8 cherry tomatoes, halved
115g/4oz firm goat's cheese, thinly sliced
handful shredded fresh basil leaves
salt and freshly ground black pepper

SERVES 4

1 Make up the pizza dough according to the directions on the packet. Roll out the dough on a lightly floured surface to a round of about 25cm/10in diameter.

4 Cook the pizza for 10 minutes more, until golden brown and crisp. Sprinkle with fresh basil and serve.

SWEET AND SOUR VEGETABLES WITH PANEER

• • •

The Indian cheese used in this recipe, called paneer, can be bought from Asian stores, or you can use tofu in its place. Paneer has a good firm texture and cooks very well on the barbecue.

INGREDIENTS

1 green pepper, cut into squares
1 yellow pepper, cut into squares
8 cherry, or 4 medium, tomatoes
8 cauliflower florets
8 fresh or canned pineapple chunks
8 cubes paneer

FOR THE SEASONED OIL
15ml/1 tbsp soya oil
30ml/2 tbsp lemon juice
5ml/1 tsp salt
5ml/1 tsp freshly ground black
pepper
15ml/1 tbsp clear honey
30ml/2 tbsp chilli sauce

SERVES 4

1 Thread the prepared vegetables, pineapple and paneer cubes on to four skewers, alternating the ingredients.

2 Mix together all the ingredients for the seasoned oil. If the mixture is a little too thick, add 15ml/1 tbsp water to loosen it. Brush the vegetables with the seasoned oil, ready for cooking.

3 Cook on a hot barbecue or grill for 10 minutes, until the vegetables begin to char slightly, turning the skewers often and basting with the seasoned oil. Serve on a bed of plain boiled rice.

VEGETABLE KEBABS WITH PEPPERCORN SAUCE

*Vegetables invariably taste good when cooked on the barbecue. You can include other
vegetables in these kebabs, depending on what is available at the time.*

INGREDIENTS

24 mushrooms
16 cherry tomatoes
16 large fresh basil leaves
2 courgettes, cut into 16 thick
slices
16 large fresh mint leaves
1 large red pepper, cut into
16 squares

TO BASTE
120ml/4fl oz/½ cup melted butter
1 garlic clove, crushed
15ml/1 tbsp crushed green
peppercorns
salt

FOR THE GREEN PEPPERCORN SAUCE
50g/2oz/¼ cup butter
45ml/3 tbsp brandy
250ml/8fl oz/1 cup double cream
5ml/1 tsp crushed green
peppercorns

SERVES 4

1 Thread the vegetables on to
8 bamboo skewers that you have
soaked in water to prevent them
burning. Place the fresh basil leaves
immediately next to the tomatoes,
and wrap the mint leaves around
the courgette slices.

2 Mix the basting ingredients in a
bowl and baste the kebabs thoroughly.
Cook the skewers on a medium-hot
barbecue, turning and basting regularly
until the vegetables are just cooked –
this should take about 5–7 minutes.

3 Heat the butter for the green
peppercorn sauce in a frying pan,
then add the brandy and light it. When
the flames have died down, stir in the
cream and the peppercorns. Cook for
2 minutes, stirring all the time. Serve
the sauce with the barbecued kebabs.

BAKED STUFFED COURGETTES

The tangy goat's cheese stuffing contrasts well with the very delicate flavour of the courgettes in this recipe. Wrap the courgettes and bake them in the embers of the fire.

2 Insert pieces of goat's cheese in the slits. Add a little chopped mint and sprinkle over the oil and black pepper.

3 Wrap each courgette in foil, place in the embers of the fire and bake for about 25 minutes, until tender.

INGREDIENTS

8 small courgettes, about 450g/1lb total weight
15ml/1 tbsp olive oil, plus extra for brushing
75–115g/3–4oz goat's cheese, cut into thin strips
a few sprigs of fresh mint, finely chopped, plus extra to garnish
freshly ground black pepper

SERVES 4

1 Cut eight pieces of baking foil large enough to encase each courgette, and lightly brush each piece with olive oil. Trim the courgettes and cut a thin slit along the length of each.

Cook's Tip
While almost any cheese can be used in this recipe, mild cheeses such as Cheddar or mozzarella, will best allow the flavour of the courgettes to be appreciated.

STUFFED PARSLEYED ONIONS

· · ·

These stuffed onions are a popular vegetarian dish served with fresh crusty bread and a crisp salad. They also make a very good accompaniment to meat dishes.

INGREDIENTS

4 large onions
60ml/4 tbsp cooked rice
20ml/4 tsp finely chopped fresh parsley, plus extra to garnish
60ml/4 tbsp strong Cheddar cheese, finely grated
30ml/2 tbsp olive oil
15ml/1 tbsp white wine
salt and freshly ground black pepper

SERVES 4

1 Cut a slice from the top of each onion and scoop out the centre to leave a fairly thick shell. Combine all the remaining ingredients in a large bowl and stir to mix, moistening with enough white wine to bind the ingredients together well.

2 Use a spoon to fill the onions, then wrap each one in a piece of oiled baking foil. Bake in the embers of the fire for 30–40 minutes, until tender, turning the parcels often so they cook evenly. Serve the onions garnished with chopped fresh parsley.

SWEETCORN IN A GARLIC BUTTER CRUST

• • •

Whether you are catering for vegetarians or serving this with meat dishes, it will disappear
in a flash. The charred garlic butter crust adds a new dimension to the corn cobs.

INGREDIENTS

6 ripe corn cobs
225g/8oz/1 cup butter
30ml/2 tbsp olive oil
2 garlic cloves, crushed
115g/4oz/1 cup wholemeal
breadcrumbs
15ml/1 tbsp chopped fresh parsley
salt and freshly ground black
pepper

SERVES 6

1 Pull off the husks and silks and boil the corn cobs in a large saucepan of salted water until tender. Drain the corn cobs and leave to cool.

2 Melt the butter in a saucepan and add the olive oil, crushed garlic, salt and freshly ground black pepper, and stir to blend. Pour the mixture into a shallow dish. In another shallow dish blend the breadcrumbs and chopped fresh parsley. Roll the corn cobs in the melted butter mixture and then in the breadcrumbs until they are well coated.

3 Cook the corn cobs on a hot barbecue for about 10 minutes, turning frequently, until the breadcrumbs are golden brown.

GRILLED AUBERGINE PARCELS

These little Italian bundles of tomatoes, mozzarella cheese and basil, wrapped in slices of aubergine, taste delicious cooked on the barbecue.

INGREDIENTS

2 large, long aubergines
225g/8oz mozzarella cheese
2 plum tomatoes
16 large fresh basil leaves
30ml/2 tbsp olive oil
salt and freshly ground black pepper

FOR THE DRESSING
60ml/4 tbsp olive oil
5ml/1 tsp balsamic vinegar
15ml/1 tbsp sun-dried tomato paste
15ml/1 tbsp lemon juice

FOR THE GARNISH
30ml/2 tbsp toasted pine nuts
torn fresh basil leaves

SERVES 4

3 Cut the mozzarella cheese into eight slices. Cut each tomato into eight slices, not counting the first and last slices. Take two aubergine slices and arrange in a cross. Place a slice of tomato in the centre, season, then add a basil leaf, followed by a slice of mozzarella, another basil leaf, another slice of tomato and more seasoning.

4 Fold the ends of the aubergine slices around the filling to make a neat parcel. Repeat with the rest of the assembled ingredients to make eight parcels. Chill the parcels in the fridge for about 20 minutes.

5 To make the tomato dressing, whisk together the olive oil, vinegar, sun-dried tomato paste and lemon juice. Season to taste with plenty of salt and freshly ground black pepper.

6 Brush the parcels with olive oil and cook on a hot barbecue for about 10 minutes, turning once, until golden. Serve hot, with the dressing, sprinkled with pine nuts and basil.

1 Remove the stalks from the aubergines and cut them lengthways into thin slices using a mandolin or long-bladed knife – aim to get 16 slices in total, each about 5mm/¼in thick, disregarding the first and last slices.

2 Bring a large saucepan of salted water to the boil and cook the aubergine slices for about 2 minutes, until just softened. Drain the slices, then pat them dry on kitchen paper.

POTATO WEDGES WITH GARLIC AND ROSEMARY

Toss the potato wedges in fragrant, garlicky olive oil with chopped fresh rosemary before barbecuing them over the coals.

INGREDIENTS

675g/1½ lb medium old potatoes
15ml/1 tbsp olive oil
2 garlic cloves, thinly sliced
60ml/4 tbsp chopped fresh rosemary
salt and freshly ground black pepper

SERVES 4

1 Cut each potato into four wedges and par-boil in boiling salted water for 5 minutes. Drain well.

2 Toss the potatoes in the olive oil with the garlic, rosemary and black pepper. Arrange on a grill rack.

3 Cook the potatoes on a hot barbecue for about 15 minutes, turning occasionally, until the wedges are crisp and golden brown.

POTATO SKEWERS WITH MUSTARD DIP
· · ·

Potatoes cooked on the barbecue have a tasty flavour and crisp skin.
These skewers are served with a thick, garlic-rich dip.

INGREDIENTS

1kg/2¼lb small new potatoes
200g/7oz/2 cups shallots, halved
30ml/2 tbsp olive oil
15ml/1 tbsp sea salt

FOR THE MUSTARD DIP
4 garlic cloves, crushed
2 egg yolks
30ml/2 tbsp lemon juice
300ml/½ pint/1¼ cups extra
virgin olive oil
10ml/2 tsp whole-grain mustard
salt and freshly ground black
pepper

SERVES 4

1 To make the mustard dip, place the garlic, egg yolks and lemon juice in a blender or food processor and process for a few seconds until smooth.

2 With the motor running, add the oil, until the mixture forms a thick cream. Add the mustard and season.

3 Par-boil the potatoes in salted boiling water for about 5 minutes. Drain well and then thread them on to metal skewers with the shallots.

4 Brush with olive oil and sprinkle with sea salt. Cook for 10–12 minutes over a hot barbecue, turning often, until tender. Serve with the mustard dip.

DESSERTS

~

SPICED PEAR AND BLUEBERRY PARCELS

This fruity combination makes a delicious dessert for a hot summer's evening.
You could substitute other berry fruits for the blueberries if you prefer.

INGREDIENTS

4 firm, ripe pears
30ml/2 tbsp lemon juice
15ml/1 tbsp melted butter
150g/5oz/1¼ cups blueberries
60ml/4 tbsp light muscovado sugar
freshly ground black pepper

SERVES 4

3 Cut four squares of double-thickness foil, large enough to wrap the pears, and brush them with melted butter. Place two pear halves on each, cut sides upwards. Gather the foil up around them, to hold them level.

4 Mix the blueberries and sugar together and spoon them over the pears. Sprinkle with black pepper. Seal the edges of the foil over the pears and cook on a fairly hot barbecue for 20–25 minutes.

1 Peel the pears thinly. Cut them in half lengthways. Scoop out the core from each half, using a teaspoon and a sharp kitchen knife.

2 Brush the pears with lemon juice, to prevent them from discolouring.

Cook's Tip

To assemble in advance, line with a layer of greaseproof paper, as the acid in the lemon juice may react with the foil and taint the flavour.

CHAR-GRILLED APPLES ON CINNAMON TOASTS

*This simple, scrumptious dessert is best made with an enriched bread such as brioche,
but any light sweet bread will do.*

INGREDIENTS

4 sweet, dessert apples
juice of ½ lemon
4 individual brioches or muffins
60ml/4 tbsp melted butter
30ml/2 tbsp golden caster sugar
5ml/1 tsp ground cinnamon
whipped cream or Greek-style
yogurt, to serve

SERVES 4

2 Cut the brioches or muffins into thick slices. Brush the slices with melted butter on both sides.

4 Place the apple and brioche slices on a medium-hot barbecue and cook them for about 3–4 minutes, turning once, until they are beginning to turn golden brown. Do not allow to burn.

1 Core the apples and use a sharp knife to cut them into 3–4 thick slices. Sprinkle the apple slices with lemon juice and set them aside.

3 Mix together the caster sugar and ground cinnamon in a small bowl to make the cinnamon sugar. Set aside.

5 Sprinkle half the cinnamon sugar over the apple slices and brioche toasts and cook for a further minute on the barbecue, until the sugar is sizzling and the toasts are a rich golden brown.

6 To serve, arrange the apple slices over the toasts and sprinkle them with the remaining cinnamon sugar. Serve hot, with whipped cream or Greek-style yogurt, if liked.

PINEAPPLE WEDGES WITH RUM BUTTER GLAZE

Fresh pineapple is even more full of flavour when barbecued, and this spiced rum glaze makes it into a very special dessert.

INGREDIENTS

1 medium pineapple
30ml/2 tbsp dark muscovado sugar
5ml/1 tsp ground ginger
60ml/4 tbsp melted butter
30ml/2 tbsp dark rum

SERVES 4

3 Soak 4 bamboo skewers in water for 15 minutes to prevent them scorching on the barbecue. Push a skewer through each wedge, into the stalk, to hold the chunks in place.

4 Mix together the sugar, ginger, butter and rum and brush over the pineapple. Cook the wedges on the barbecue for 4 minutes; pour the remaining glaze over the top and serve.

1 With a large, sharp knife, cut the pineapple lengthways into four wedges. Cut out and discard the central core.

2 Cut between the flesh and skin, to release the skin, but leave the flesh in place. Slice the flesh across and lengthways to make thick chunks.

Cook's Tip

For an easier version, simply remove the skin and then cut the whole pineapple into thick slices and cook as above.

NECTARINES WITH MARZIPAN AND MASCARPONE

A luscious dessert that no one can resist – dieters may prefer to use low-fat soft cheese or ricotta instead of mascarpone.

INGREDIENTS

4 firm, ripe nectarines or peaches
75g/3oz marzipan
75g/3oz/5 tbsp mascarpone cheese
3 macaroon biscuits, crushed

SERVES 4

1 Cut the nectarines or peaches in half and remove the stones.

2 Divide the marzipan into eight pieces, roll into balls, using your fingers, and press one piece of marzipan into the stone cavity of each nectarine half.

Cook's Tip

Either nectarines or peaches can be used for this recipe. If the stone does not pull out easily when you halve the fruit, use a small, sharp knife to cut around it.

3 Spoon the mascarpone cheese on top of the fruit halves. Sprinkle the crushed macaroon bicuits over the mascarpone cheese.

4 Place the half-fruits on a hot barbecue for 3–5 minutes, until they are hot and the mascarpone starts to melt. Serve immediately.

ORANGES IN MAPLE AND COINTREAU SYRUP

This is one of the most delicious ways to eat an orange, and a luxurious way to round off a barbecued meal. For a children's or alcohol-free version, omit the liqueur.

INGREDIENTS

20ml/4 tsp butter, plus extra, melted, for brushing
4 medium oranges
30 ml/2 tbsp maple syrup
30ml/2 tbsp Cointreau or Grand Marnier liqueur
crème fraîche or fromage frais, to serve

SERVES 4

2 Remove some shreds of orange rind, to decorate. Blanch these, dry them and set them aside. Peel the oranges, removing all the white pith and catching the juice in a bowl.

4 Tuck the baking foil up securely around the oranges to keep them in shape, leaving the foil open at the top.

1 Cut four double-thickness squares of baking foil, large enough to wrap each of the oranges. Brush the centre of each square of foil with plenty of melted butter.

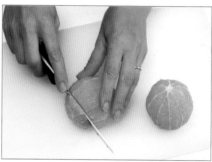

3 Slice the oranges crossways into thick slices. Reassemble them and place each orange on a square of baking foil.

5 Mix together the reserved orange juice, maple syrup and liqueur and spoon the mixture over the oranges.

6 Add a knob of butter to each parcel and close the foil at the top to seal in the juices. Place the parcels on a hot barbecue for 10–12 minutes, until hot. Serve with crème fraîche or fromage frais, topped with the reserved shreds of orange rind.

INDEX

. . .